SRI SRI PARAMAHANSA YOGANANDA
Gurudeva and Founder
Yogoda Satsanga Society of India/
Self-Realization Fellowship

DEVELOPING DYNAMIC WILL

and Other Lectures

By
Sri Sri Paramahansa Yogananda

"He is the wisest who seeks God. He is the most successful who has found God."
— *Sri Sri Paramahansa Yogananda*

Copyright © 1980, 2002 Self-Realization Fellowship

All rights reserved. Except for brief quotations in book reviews and as otherwise permitted by applicable law, no part of this work may be reproduced, stored, transmitted or displayed in any form, or by any means (electronic, mechanical, or otherwise) now known or hereafter devised — including photocopy, recording, or any information storage and retrieval system — without prior written permission from Self-Realization Fellowship, 3880 San Rafael Avenue, Los Angeles, California 90065-3219, U.S.A.

First Indian Edition, 1980
Seventh Impression, 2012

 An authorized publication of Yogoda Satsanga Society of India / Self-Realization Fellowship

The trade dress of this book is a trademark of Self-Realization Fellowship

Published in India by
YOGODA SATSANGA SOCIETY OF INDIA
Yogoda Satsanga Math
21, U. N. Mukherjee Road
Dakshineswar, Kolkata 700076

Printed in India by
Annapurna Press & Process
Ranchi-834001

ISBN 978-81-89535-29-2

Distributed by:

 Jaico Publishing House

Also available from Yogoda Satsanga Society of India, Paramahansa Yogananda Path, Ranchi 834001, Jharkhand and at Yogoda Satsanga Ashrams and Dhyana Kendras throughout India.

PREFACE

From the embryonic period of man's reason he has sought to understand the mysteries of his existence and the nature of his Creator. Enlightenment on these matters has been the special mission of wise men in every age. Realizing this, the ideal of *satsanga* (company with the good and the wise) has rooted itself in the very core of India's spiritual tradition. From *satsanga* the *sadhak* gathers inspiration and advances his spiritual understanding. The more divine the good company is, the more the *sadhak* can absorb from the experience. But only a fortunate few have the rare and blessed opportunity to be actually in the personal company of a truly great soul. The seeking masses are denied this privilege if we take literally the concept of *satsanga* as the necessity to be in the physical presence of the saint. If, however, we realize that the intrinsic value of *satsanga* is in the ability of the devotee to be receptive to the teachings and guidance of the saint, whether or not the *sadhak* be in the physical company of that divine soul, the modern medium of the printed word brings the upliftment of *satsanga* to the *sadhana* of every seeker.

It is in this spirit that *Developing Dynamic Will* is offered to the reader.

Sri Sri Paramahansa Yogananda, who speaks to you in the pages of this booklet, entered mahasamadhi on March 7, 1952. The remarkable incorruptibility of his body after death was a continued reflection of his unique, spiritually transcendent life. He is the revered Guru-founder of the now worldwide institution of Yogoda Satsanga Society of India/Self-Realization Fellowship. The basis of his teaching is *Raja Yoga*, the ancient, universal science of soul-realization. The Society carries on its activities and spreads the teachings of Sri Sri Paramahansa Yogananda through publication of his books and writings, including confidential spiritual lessons; and through the medium of branch centers, and educational and charitable institutions. If this booklet is the reader's first introduction to Paramahansa Yoganandaji and the Society he founded, the experience of *satsanga* with the blessed Guru in these pages may well be the beginning of a deeper acquaintance and continuing relationship.

The worth of any writing consists in its ability to convey the intended message; the authority of the message lies in the qualifications of the writer. The contents of this booklet will speak for itself; the authority of the author is readily confirmed by a thoughtful perusal of *Autobiography of a Yogi,* the life testimony of one to whom Truth was not fact but realization.

The Publishers
YOGODA SATSANGA SOCIETY OF INDIA

The Spiritual Legacy of
Sri Sri Paramahansa Yogananda

A century after the birth of Paramahansa Yogananda, he has come to be recognized as one of the preeminent spiritual figures of our time; and the influence of his life and work continues to grow. Many of the religious and philosophical concepts and methods he introduced decades ago are now finding expression in education, psychology, business, medicine, and other spheres of endeavor — contributing in far-reaching ways to a more integrated, humane, and spiritual vision of human life.

The fact that Paramahansa Yoganandaji's teachings are being interpreted and creatively applied in many different fields and by exponents of diverse philosophical and metaphysical movements, points not only to the great practical utility of what he taught, but also to the need for some means of ensuring that the spiritual legacy he left not be diluted, fragmented, or distorted with the passing of time.

With the increasing variety of sources of information about Paramahansa Yogananda, readers sometimes inquire how they can be certain that a publication accurately presents his life and teachings. In response to these inquiries, we would like to explain that Paramahansaji founded Yogoda Satsanga Society of India/Self-Realization Fellowship to disseminate his teachings and to preserve their purity and integrity for future generations. He personally chose and trained those close disciples who head the Yogoda Satsanga Society of India/Self-Realization Fellowship Publications Council, and gave them specific guidelines for the preparation and publishing of his lectures, writings, and *Yogoda Satsanga Lessons*. The members of the YSS/SRF Publications Council honor these guidelines as a sacred trust, in order that the universal message of this beloved world teacher may live on in its original power and authenticity.

The Yogoda Satsanga Society of India/Self-Realization Fellowship name and the YSS/SRF emblem (shown above) were originated by Paramahansaji to identify the organization he founded to carry on his worldwide spiritual and humanitarian work. These appear on all YSS/SRF books, audio and video recordings, films, and other publications, assuring the reader that the work originates with the organization founded by Sri Sri Paramahansa Yogananda and faithfully conveys his teachings as he himself intended they be given.

—Yogoda Satsanga Society of India/
Self-Realization Fellowship

CONTENTS

PREFACE iii

1. DEVELOPING DYNAMIC WILL 1

2. OVERCOMING MALIGNANT MOODS 16

3. DEVELOPING PERSONALITY 27

4. ELIMINATING THE STATIC OF FEAR

    FROM THE MIND RADIO 35

Developing Dynamic Will

*Self-Realization Fellowship International Headquarters,
Los Angeles, California, January 11, 1949*

God sent man on earth empowered with certain physical, mental, and spiritual forces that he can wield, and, by their wise use, produce intended definite results. The force that runs machinery is electricity. And this complex human machine that God has given us, a movable structure of bones covered with tender flesh and consisting of trillions of cells, is run by *prana*, intelligent life force, traveling like electricity through the wires of the nerves.

In childhood the body is more responsive to the mind; it can more easily make the body do its bidding. But later on, as the child develops various habits, the body and mind do not work in the same harmony as before. Although, as I have often pointed out, the material form is only a dream in the consciousness of God, so long as you have to use the physical body, it should be under the control of your mind.

Troubles will always strike at the body, for this is a law of life; in spite of difficulties, you should keep such mental neutrality that the mind is not affected by outer conditions.

St. Francis of Assisi suffered terribly, yet he was mentally unaffected. Shortly before his death he was going blind. The doctor advised a treatment that required cauterization of the saint's face, from the eyebrows back to the ears, with a white-hot iron bar. There were no anesthetics then. The disciples present could not bear the sight, but St. Francis told the physician to proceed with the treatment. He welcomed Brother Fire with sweet words and never showed that he felt even the slightest connection between the mind and the body. The Lord wants you also to understand this truth: that within your perishable body is an inviolable, immortal soul.

It is an error to suppose that masters do not suffer at all. Jesus let his body suffer the pains of crucifixion, even though he was already redeemed, for he thereby willingly worked out on his own body some of the karmic suffering due his disciples and the world. But he knew the relationship between mind and body; he saw them as a delusory creation in the cosmic dream of God. The body is merely a cluster of sensations. It is not easy to cut off sensations, but you can do so by remaining constantly in the consciousness that you are a soul, one with Spirit. When the mind is almost wholly dominated by the body and its demands, as is the case with most persons, it is best to begin gradually, in little things, to dissociate the mind from the body.

One difference between an ordinary man and a superman is that the ordinary man cries and gives in to suffering if he is hurt, but the yogi is established in the consciousness that he is not the body, that he is apart from it. This realization is with me all the time. Sometimes I see myself walking, and I am simultaneously aware that I have no body. In the divine consciousness you realize that you, as soul, have no hands, eyes, ears, or feet, nor any need of these physical adjuncts; yet you can use and move these bodily instruments. It is possible to hear, see, smell, taste, and touch with mind power alone. In clairaudience, for example, one hears through the power within. Many

Developing Dynamic Will

saints hear the voice of God or one of His angels guiding them. They hear not with ears but with mind. Such a state of consciousness is a real experience, not imagination. But it cannot become your experience unless you meditate. If you meditate with the greatest devotion, someday when you least expect it you will have the same experience, and you will understand what I am speaking of.

God is constantly showing me this truth, that the body is unreal. He has also shown me that this body shall suffer. But the physical suffering this body will endure has nothing to do with my consciousness. It comes from taking on the negative *karma* of others, and has no connection with misery-producing desires of self. If this body does some good to the world and to others, fine. A master does not care what happens to his body. He just looks after it that others may be benefited.

The only time the ordinary person is not conscious of the body is during sleep; yet upon waking, he is immediately conscious of how well or poorly he slept. Some materialists think that we are wholly unconscious when we are asleep, but this is not true. How could we know, upon waking, how well or ill we slept, unless we were conscious during sleep? We can safely say that the mind can exist without the body.

Wisdom and Will Govern Body and Mind

What, then, are the principal powers that govern body and mind? Wisdom and will. Wisdom is the soul's intuitive, direct knowledge of truth. During warfare, range finders are used to determine where to fire shells; once the range is found, the guns are effectively fired. Wisdom is your range finder, and your will gives the firing power to accomplish your ends according to the dictates of your wisdom. Your will should always be guided by wisdom. One without the other is dangerous. If you have wisdom but not sufficient will to follow through as wisdom dictates, it is hurtful to your well-being; if you have a strong will but no wisdom, there is every chance of "misfiring" and destroying yourself.

Your intelligence is not guided by true wisdom if it fails to show you the right thing that you should do. And, if it doesn't encourage the strength of will necessary to carry out the behests of your soul, then that power of intelligence is not fulfilling its true purpose. "The senses are said to be superior (to the physical body); the mind is superior to the sense faculties; the intelligence is superior to the mind; and the one that is superior to the intellect is He (the real Self, the soul)."*

Most people are like automatons. They breakfast, go to work, have lunch, go back to work, come home to dinner, watch TV, and go to bed; then the body machine is shut off for the night. Those who live in this way are using only mechanical will, performing most of their actions as a matter of habit, accomplishing their duties always in a certain way. They make little or no effort to exercise their will consciously. True, they are using will power all the time in performing these habitual actions, but it is purely mechanical; it is not *dynamic* will.

Physiological Will — First Expression of Will Power

When human beings are born, the initial expression of will power is the baby's first cry, which opens up the lungs and

---

* Bhagavad-Gita III:42

Developing Dynamic Will

causes breathing to begin. Sages say that the soul doesn't like being caged in the feeble little baby body; its first experience in that form is to cry. The soul realizes that in the human form it will again go through many struggles, and says, "Lord, why did you put me here again?" Many babies' hands are folded at birth. Their soul is worshiping God in this way and praying, "O Spirit, release me in this life."

Will is a tremendous factor in life. It is the power by which you can reach the heights of God-realization, or go down into the deepest strata of ignorance. The cry of a newborn child is an expression of physiological will; the baby wills to remove the discomfort it feels. Most people have not risen above that state of babyhood. They immediately want to be rid of any discomfort, and whenever they see anything that attracts them, they cry for it. They think they have got to have it, that they can't live without it. The will that is thus overpowered by the senses is called physiological will — body-bound will, following the dictates of the senses.

It is terrible to use any kind of drug, for the drug enslaves the will to the body. I once knew a man who used opium. All day long he slept in a stupor. It took him years to overcome his slavery. To use narcotics is one of the greatest sins against Spirit. Drink is the same. Both mean destruction of will power. The great saints have warned against them. Under no circumstance should you let yourself be tempted, for in a short while you can be lost. Drink and drugs are sins against the soul because they paralyze the will, without which soul-realization and salvation are impossible.

Many people are bound by physiological will. The very

power that governs *prana* and enables it to efficiently operate the human machine is destroyed when strong habits of sex or drink or hatred take over. And once they are established they are very difficult to conquer. Once you are in the habit of showing temper whenever you are crossed, you follow that habit in spite of your wish to behave otherwise. Habit destroys the supreme gift of heaven — will power — by which you can work out your own salvation.

Without Wisdom, Will Becomes Habit-Bound

If God and heaven were imposed on us, then we would be their slaves. But the Lord has given us free choice by which we can accept good or cast it out, accept evil or cast it out. The powers that God has given you by which you can make this choice are wisdom and will. Find out whether you have control over your will or not. Don't let your will be devitalized by bad habits.

After physiological will comes habit-bound will. Your will automatically enters this second phase unless it is guided by wisdom. Sometimes a good man's child is lacking in truthfulness and good habits. Certainly the child has had every opportunity to learn to be good; yet the moment he becomes old enough to start using his own will, he gets into all kinds of mischief. Why? Usually in such cases the child's nature from past lives is karmically inclined toward wrong thinking and habits. Through his family training in this life he learns to perform good actions; but they are only superimposed on his real nature. Because his will is controlled only by mechanical good habits, rather than by soul

Developing Dynamic Will

wisdom and true understanding, he readily succumbs to temptations when he is free of the good influence of the family.

If you ask thieves and habitual drinkers if they like their way of life, they usually say "No." They thought when they started their wrong actions that they would be happy. They never realized that the effects would be hurtful to them. For this reason I deeply feel for people who have done wrong. I cry for them. "But for the grace of God, there go I." Evil is a sort of opiate. That is why we should have places where people who have gone wrong can learn how to live and how to think. Jail is not a suitable place of reform. Such persons need to mix with superior men who can help them.

All around you are thieves of circumstances, trying to steal your vitality of will; but no one can take away your will but yourself. The child wants his own way. When he grows up, unless his will has been curbed and guided by wisdom, he finds that he is a slave to desires. Are you not doing things today that you know you ought not to do, and which you know will bring you unhappiness later on? Overstimulation of the senses devitalizes the will, so do not create an unnatural craving for anything. Suppose you like a certain food very much. Your will power should be such that you can do without it henceforth.

It is impossible to say what you really like and don't like, because your inclinations are always changing. If you analyze yourself you will see that in the matter of likes and dislikes we are all crazy. We don't know why we like certain things and don't like others. What you like through the influence of your wisdom, and what you like as a result of your physiological habits, are two different things. I can make myself like something, and the next minute I can make myself repelled by it.

To be guided by wisdom is to be king of the world. The wise man tries first to determine if he is right; then he acts. But if he makes a decision and then finds out he was wrong, he immediately acknowledges his mistake. Never use your will power to be stubborn. You can talk with some people for an hour, and they seemingly agree with you, and then they turn around and say just the opposite. They don't want to give up their own way. That is not will power, but slavery to the ego. You can see such slaves all around you. They think they are free, but their will is chained; they perform actions mechanically, guided by good or by evil habits. But when you can say, "I stay away from evil because evil works against my happiness," or "I am good, not because I am forced to be, but because good leads to my own happiness" — that is wisdom. Such was my guru's training. One thing we should always remember: If will is guided by wisdom, it will produce something constructive in our life.

When Jesus said to the Heavenly Father, "Thy will be done,"* it was not because he lacked will power, but because he wanted his will to be guided by God's. When the Divine Will intimated, "Give up the body," Jesus had to use a great deal of will power to conquer the weakness of the flesh. Human will has become divine will, completely attuned to Spirit, when even though it is necessary to give up the body, one is able to do so willingly, as Christ did. A body-bound

---

* Matthew 26:42.

SRI SRI MAHAVATAR BABAJI
Guru of Sri Sri Lahiri Mahasaya

SRI SRI LAHIRI MAHASAYA
(Shyama Charan Lahiri)
Guru of Sri Sri Swami
Sri Yukteswar Giri

**SRI SRI SWAMI
SRI YUKTESWAR GIRI**
Guru of Sri Sri
Paramahansa Yogananda

SRI SRI DAYA MATA
Sanghamata and President of
Yogoda Satsanga Society of India/
Self-Realization Fellowship

slave would have said, "They are trying to crucify me; I must try to save myself." If Jesus had done that, he would not have been the Christ who lives in our hearts today.

Stages of Will Development

Man progresses from the physiological will of infancy to the unthinking will of childhood. That is when he is used to obeying his mother, doing whatever she tells him to do. After unthinking will comes blind will; he gets away from the mother's will and begins to feel his own will power. This comes in youth. He tests his own will and begins to use it to get what he sets his heart on.

As a child I wanted a bicycle and I got it. Then I wanted a horse, but I didn't get it. A long time after, though, I did receive it. Every desire that I have had has been satisfied by the Lord. Everything I have wished for has come to me. That was His blessing.

I was always careful that my wish was right before I used my will to carry it out. It is good to be stubborn in good things, but never otherwise. When you are wrong, you should correct yourself. If you don't blind yourself to good by using your will for wrong things, then you progress from blind will to thinking will.

After Mother died, when I was only eleven years old, and so grief-stricken! my eldest sister Roma loved to guide me. Others tried to use force, but Roma won me by love. Even when I was obstinately saying to her, "Go away, go away," I found myself obeying her wishes.

The nature of a saint is tender like a flower, but stronger than thunder when he makes up his mind about something good, because his will is guided by wisdom. It was not the easiest thing to convince my guru when I felt I had a better idea, but as soon as he saw that I offered a different angle he would say: "You are right. Let us do it that way." But when I was wrong, he couldn't be moved.

Thinking will is the most marvelous instrument you can imagine. Are you governed by thinking will, or by blind will, or by physiological will? Thinking will is the way toward wisdom. When you get a notion in your mind that you must go to the movies, that is physiological will. And when you decide, "Well, it doesn't matter, I will go some other time," that is thinking will.

Will that is not guided by habit is thinking will. If you don't want to smoke, you should not smoke. If you do not feel hungry, don't eat just because of habit. Whenever I wish to refrain from taking food, no one can tempt me to eat. Another habit amongst those hardest to control is that of harsh speech. Speaking unkindly to others paralyzes your will. Never be cranky. Whenever you get angry you make your face ugly. Be so loving and kind that everyone who meets you says of you, "I would like to see that person again." When you control your own speech you will not be so sensitive to others' remarks about you. I quit anger when I was a little child. But I often discipline with strong words those understanding ones whom God has sent me for training. To those who don't understand, I never say anything.

See how wonderful will power is. After you have developed thinking will, you begin to reason, "I must produce something worthwhile with this power," and you take up one

Developing Dynamic Will

thing at a time and try to accomplish it. You revolve that will around a problem of health or of finances or of controlling a habit, or around the desire to know God. If you will and act until victory, then you have attained dynamic will.

The World Will Try to Trick You

Everything in life tempts you away from God. In the beginning most devotees fall down, because they don't use their divine will; they put off meditation. Day after day, week after week, they put it off. You know you want to love God, you know you ought to get busy making the effort now, and still you procrastinate. I remember a period in my childhood when I lost a great deal of time in this manner. I was already meditating every day, and I had resolved to meditate much longer each day. But I kept putting it off until suddenly I realized a whole year had gone by. Then I remembered the story about the cat and the sparrow.

The cat caught a sparrow, but the sparrow was wise. He reminded the cat that it was proper first to lick clean his face and paws in preparation for the sparrow meal. This made sense to the cat, so he let the sparrow go and took his time washing himself. In the meantime the sparrow flew away to a high branch. The cat finally said, "You can come down now. I am ready for my dinner." But the sparrow chirped, "Too bad; I am now at the top of the tree." So the cat resolved: "Henceforth, I will eat my sparrow first and then wash myself."

First things must come first. When you awaken in the morning, meditate. If you don't, the whole world will crowd in to claim you, and you will forget God. At night, meditate before sleep claims you. I am so strongly established in the habit of meditation that even after I lie down to sleep at night, I find I am meditating. I can't sleep in the ordinary way. The habit of being with God comes first.

In Your Will Power Lies the Image of God

Will power means freedom. Will power means Heaven. If you don't permit your will to be weakened by the attractions of the world, you will reach your divine goal. But most of you have allowed your will to be sapped by bad habits — many of you indulge in them every day — smoking, drinking, angry speech. You think you can't do without these things. But there was a time when you didn't know what smoke was, or what drink was, or what anger was. You have given up your freedom by acquiring these habits. Must you remain a slave to them? How can you find God unless you free your will power, by eliminating these worldly habits and by using that will to meditate instead?

No matter what happens to your body, meditate. Never go to sleep at night until you have communed with God. Your body will remind you that you have worked hard and need rest, but the more you ignore its demands and concentrate on the Lord, the more you will burn with joyous life, like a globe afire. Then you will know that you are not the body. In your will power lies the image of God. That image has been desecrated because you have made a slave of your mind. When I left India to come to America, my guru said: "Forget you were born among Hindus, and don't adopt all the ways of the Americans .... Be your true self, a child of God." By following his wise advice, I have kept my will free. If the whole world stood against me, and I saw that I was right and others were wrong, I would not change my mind.

Nothing Is Impossible
When Will Becomes Dynamic

Choose a good, wholesome, constructive goal and then determine that you are going to achieve it. No matter how many times you fail, keep on trying. No matter what happens, if you have unalterably resolved, "The earth may be shattered, but I will keep on doing the best I can," you are using dynamic will, and you will succeed. That dynamic will is what makes one man rich and another man strong and another man a saint.

It is not Jesus and a few others who alone know God. If you make the right kind of effort, *you* will find God. What is the value of using dynamic will today to be a great doctor, or a successful businessman, when tomorrow you may die? This is why Jesus said, "Seek ye first the kingdom of God."* Use your will to know God first; then He will direct your path in life.

You are using dynamic will when day and night you whisper within, "Lord, Lord, Lord," with the deepest desire to find Him. It is better to use your will to seek God than for anything else. I am so happy that He blessed me with the divine will power that my guru, Sri Yukteswarji, awakened in me. Before I met Master I was exercising that will power right and left in useless things. But even then, whenever I started something, I employed dynamic will to complete it.

I remember the first time I used dynamic will to help others. My friend and I were just little boys then. One day I said to

---

* Matthew 6:33.

him, "We are going to feed five hundred people."

"But we haven't a paisa!" he exclaimed. "We are going to do it just the same," I assured him. "And I think the money is going to come through you."

"That is impossible!" he scoffed. An intuitive conviction prompted me to say: "Don't offend your mother in any way. Do whatever she asks you to do."

One day later he came running and told me this story. "I was bathing and Mother called me. I was going to say, 'Don't bother me now while I am bathing,' but instead I asked her what she wanted. She told me to go and see my aunt who lived nearby. I said, 'All right.'

"When I went to see my aunt, the first thing she said to me was, 'Who is this crazy boy you are mixing with? Have you lost your mind? What is this I hear about your feeding five hundred people?' I was angry with her. 'I must leave now,' I told her, and started to go. But she stopped me, saying, 'Your friend may be crazy, but his idea is good. Here are twenty rupees.'"

The boy had nearly fainted with surprise. He ran to me at once to tell me the news. When we went to buy the rice and other things, the people in the neighborhood had already heard of our plan, and added more food. In the end we fed two thousand people! The same divinely charged will power also brought about the first library I founded, Saraswat Library in Calcutta.

When you make up your mind to do good things, you will accomplish them if you use dynamic will power to follow through. No matter what the circumstances are, if you go on trying, God will create the means by which your will shall find its proper reward. This is the truth Jesus referred to when he

Developing Dynamic Will

said: "If ye have faith, and doubt not, ... if ye shall say unto this mountain, Be thou removed, and be thou cast into the sea, it shall be done."* If you continuously use your will power, no matter what reverses come, it will produce success and health and power to help people, and above all, it will produce communion with God.

This is the kind of will power you must develop — the will power that will run the ocean dry if necessary in order to accomplish what is good. The greatest will should be used to meditate. The Lord wants us to discover our divine will and use it to find Him. Develop this God-seeking dynamic will. It is not profound words that will give you emancipation, but your own efforts through meditation.

* Matthew 21:21.

Overcoming Malignant Moods

First Self-Realization Fellowship Temple at Encinitas, California, March 5, 1939

Moods are not easily defined; but you know what they are. When you are in a mood, your behavior is not natural; you are not the person you should be. The end result is that you feel wretched. And how foolish it is to be unhappy through your own doing! Nobody *likes* misery. Why not analyze yourself next time you are in a mood? You will see how you are willingly, willfully making yourself miserable. And while you are doing so, others around you feel the unpleasantness of your state of mind. Wherever you go, you tell about yourself without speaking, because your whole mood carries its vibrations in your eyes, and anyone looking at you is aware of the negativity recorded there. Seeing the dark feelings reflected in your eyes, others are repelled; they want to stay away from those discomforting vibrations. You must remove moods from your mental mirror before you can remove their reflection from your eyes.

We Live in a Glass House

You are living in the glass house of this world, and everyone else is watching you. You cannot pose, you have to live a natural life. So why not behave in such a way that others will look up to you? Why should they not see joy in your face? All your good qualities are covered up inside by your moodiness.

Not only are others observing how you conduct yourself; you also are studying how they behave. Because you tend to make comparisons as a result of constantly watching those around you, you fall into moods. Or you may become moody over the endless difficulties one encounters in this world. Moods are often a result of environmental influences. Each one of us is affected in different ways by the world about us. But you should not allow yourself to indulge in moods over external conditions. Why should you take on the effects of your environment? There are people who resort to moods in an attempt to avoid facing some problem. But moodiness is neither an escape nor an emotional safety valve. It is natural now and then to fall momentarily into a mood; but don't hold on to it!

Each type of mood has a specific cause, and it lies within your own mind. To remove a mood you must remove its cause. One should introspect each day in order to understand the nature of his mood, and how to correct it, if it is a harmful one. Perhaps you find yourself in an indifferent state of mind. No matter what is suggested, you are not interested. It is necessary then to make a conscious effort to create some positive interest. Beware of indifference, which ossifies your progress in life by paralyzing your will power.

Perhaps your mood is discouragement over sickness; a feeling that you will never regain health. You must try to apply the laws of right living that lead to a healthy, active, and moral life, and pray for greater faith in the healing power of God.

Or suppose your mood is a conviction that you are a failure, and can never succeed at anything. Analyze the problem and see if you have really made all the effort you could have.

Consider the hard work of the president of the United States. He has to try to please all the forty-eight states,* and other nations as well. We have to marvel that it is possible for a man to understand so much and undertake so much. And as there is such a difference between the working capacity of the ordinary man and that of the president, how much greater the difference between that of the president and God, who is infinitely busier! God is managing the whole universe, down to the most minute detail — *and we are made in His image.* Therefore we cannot make excuses for failure to succeed. Don't be afraid of hard work; it has never hurt anyone. However, one should learn to work — and to think — calmly. When you are calmly active you can accomplish anything you set out to do, for the mind is clear.

In addition to not working hard enough for success, most people are not mentally active enough. They spend too much time not thinking. It is considered to be relaxation. However, in true relaxation one is calmly active mentally; he may reflect about God, or about a beautiful peaceful scene, or about some pleasant experience. Calm, positive mental activity is revivifying. Yet many people wrongly associate creative effort with strain, and go about it with a tense, nervous attitude.

Moods Get Their Grip on a Vacant Mind

Creative thinking is the best antidote for moods. Moods get their grip on your consciousness when you are in a negative or passive state of mind. The time when your mind is vacant is

---

* Alaska and Hawaii were not yet states at the time Paramahansaji made this observation. *(Publisher's Note)*

just the time it can become moody; and when you are moody, the devil comes and wields his influence on you. Therefore, develop creative thinking. Whenever you are not active physically, do something creative in your mind. Keep it so busy that you have no time to indulge in moodiness.

Creative thinking is marvelous — like living in another world. Everyone should develop this power. I think hardly a word of my lecture before I come here; but I get into the consciousness of my subject, and my soul begins to tell me wonderful things. When you are thinking creatively, you don't feel the body or moods; you become attuned with Spirit. Our human intelligence is made in the image of His creative intelligence, through which all things are possible; and if we don't live in that consciousness, we become a bundle of moods. By thinking creatively we destroy those moods; and by thinking creatively we will find all the answers to our problems, and to the problems of others.

Moods are like cancer — they eat into the peace of the soul. That is why the moody man cannot rid himself of his troubles. Remember: no matter how wrong everything has gone for you, you have no right to be moody. In your *mind* you can be a conqueror. When bested, the moody man admits defeat. But the man whose mind remains unconquered, though the world be in cinders at his feet, is yet the victor.

Do you want to be a prisoner or a conqueror? By binding yourself so tightly in moods, you render yourself incapable of going on with the battle of life. As soon as you allow a mood to enwrap your mind, your will becomes paralyzed. Moods befog the brain, and hence impair judgment, so that your efforts are wasted.

Moods Are the Brakes on Your Wheels of Progress

You can conquer your moods, no matter how terrible they seem. Make up your mind that you are not going to be moody anymore; and if a mood comes in spite of your resolve, analyze the cause that brought it on, and do something constructive about it. Don't go on doing things in a state of indifference, if that is your attitude, for indifference is the worst of all moods. At such times, remind yourself that you are not your own creator; God created you, and He is running this universe for you. Whatever your work, do it enthusiastically, for Him. Busy yourself in creative activities, for He has given you infinite power. How dare you make yourself a mental failure by indulgence in the intoxicant of moodiness! Free yourself from these devastating mental states. They are the real brakes on the wheels of your progress. Until you release them, you cannot move on. Every morning, remind yourself that you are God's child, and that no matter what the difficulties, you have the power to overcome them. Heir to the cosmic power of Spirit, you are more dangerous than danger!

An intelligent boy does not care to work on simple problems; he enjoys the challenge of difficult ones. But many people are afraid of life's problems. I have never feared them, for I have always prayed: "Lord, may Thy power increase in me. Keep me in the positive consciousness that with Thy help I can always overcome my difficulties." Think constructively about a problem till you cannot think anymore. When I am solving a problem, I go to the nth degree to cover all possible steps toward its solution, until I can honestly say: "I have done my best, and that is all I can do." Then I forget it.

A person who keeps the worry of a problem in his consciousness becomes moody. Avoid that. When a problem comes up, instead of dwelling on it, think of every possible avenue of action to rid yourself of it. If you are unable to think, compare your particular trouble with others, similar troubles, and from their experiences learn which ways lead to failure and which ways lead to success. Choose those steps that seem logical and practical, and then get busy implementing them. The whole library of the universe is hidden within you. All the things you want to know are within yourself. To bring them out, think creatively.

Magical Effect of Sincere Love

Moods blunt one's feelings and understanding, making it impossible to get along with others. Domestic life should be a temple of heaven, but moods can make it a hades. A husband comes home and finds his wife in a sullen mood, and he can't reason with her. Or he returns from work in a nasty mood, and she can't reason with him. So much trouble comes to people because of moods!

When someone else in your family is seething with anger, or is wholly indifferent, you are affected immediately by his mood. Or perhaps you go to someone in great joy, but he is moody and quarrelsome, and finally he gives you a slap. Immediately your joy vanishes, and you want to retaliate. Do not put on the mood of another. The Bible tells us that if anyone smites us on the left cheek, we should turn the right cheek. How many do that? More often, the person slapped wants to give his assailant twelve slaps in reprisal — and perhaps a kick, or even a bullet! It is easy to strike back, but to give love is the highest way to try to disarm your persecutor. Even if it doesn't work at the time, he will never be able to forget that when he gave you a slap, you gave love in return. That love must be sincere; when it comes from the heart, love is magical. You should not look for the effects; even if your love is spurned, pay no attention. Give love and forget. Don't expect anything; then you will see the magical result.

Do you realize that within you, in your soul, is a superb garden? A wondrous garden of thoughts, fragrant with love, goodness, understanding, and peace, and more beautiful than any earthly flowers that grow. You cultivated a fragrant blossom whenever someone in anger misunderstood you and you continuously gave love to him. Isn't the aroma of that love and understanding more lasting than that of any rose? So always think of your mind as a garden, and keep it beautiful and fragrant with divine thoughts; let it not become a mud pond, rank with malodorous hateful moods. If you cultivate the heavenly scented blooms of peace and love, the bee of Christ Consciousness* will steal into your garden. As the bee seeks out only those flowers that are sweet with honey, so God comes only when your life is sweet with honeyed thoughts. Resolve that in your garden of good soul qualities you will not allow the evil stinkweed of anger to grow. The more you develop flower-like divine qualities, the more God will reveal to you His secret omnipresence in your soul.

"He who is tranquil before friend and foe alike, and in (encountering) adoration and insult, and during the experiences of warmth and chill and of pleasure and suffering ... that

---

* God's omnipresent intelligence, and the attractive force of His love, manifested in creation.

person is very dear to Me."* By continuously giving love to those who are unkind, peace to those who are harassed by worries, sweetness to those who are bitter, joy to those who are laden with miseries; and by constantly setting a better example for those who follow the path of error, you destroy moods by keeping the mind creatively busy. If you can't be busy outwardly, be constructively busy inwardly.

Live in a World of Wonder

I often say: If you read for one hour, write for two hours; and if you write for two hours, think for three hours; and if you think for three hours, meditate all the time. God is the repository of all happiness; and you can contact Him in everyday life. Yet man mostly occupies himself in pursuits that lead to unhappiness. Meditation is the best way to destroy moods and live in a world of wonder — a world such as Narada, a great *rishi,* knew when he said: "Lord, I was singing Thy praises, and became lost in Thee. When I came back to this consciousness, I saw that I had slipped from my old body, and You had given me a new one!"

A similar story is told in India about another saint. A young man had just died. His body had been carried to the cremation grounds and the mourners were preparing to light the fire, when suddenly an old man came running, crying out, "Stop! Don't do it, I will use that body." As soon as he said this, the man's aged body dropped lifeless to the ground, and the young man got up from the pyre and ran off toward the forest. The old man was a great saint; he had simply not wished to interrupt his devotions by taking rebirth in an infant's helpless body.

* Bhagavad-Gita XII:18-19.

Fear Enters When God Is Shut Out of Life

There are so many wondrous things to know about life and death, and meditation is the way. Learn to live in this world as a son of God. Death holds terror for man because he has left God out of his life. All painful things frighten us, because we love the world without understanding its mystery and purpose. But when we behold everything as God, we have nothing to fear. We are constantly "born" in life as well as death. The word "death" is a great misnomer, for there is no death; when you are tired of life, you simply take off the overcoat of flesh and go back to the astral world.*

Death means an end. A car whose parts are worn out is dead; it has come to an end. And so at death the physical body comes to an end. But the immortal soul cannot be dead. Every night, in sleep, the soul lives without any consciousness of the physical body; but it is not dead. Death is only a greater sleep, wherein the soul lives in the astral body without the consciousness of the physical body. If loss of physical-body consciousness signified death for man, then the soul would die when we go to sleep. But we are not dead when we are asleep; nor are we completely unconscious, because when we awaken, we remember whether we slept well or not. So, in the afterstate of death we do not die.

Those who allow their minds to ossify are truly dying. To solve

---

* The Hindu scriptures state that the soul of man is encased successively in three bodies: the idea or causal body, a subtle astral body, and a gross physical body. The astral world is the subtle realm of finer forces to which the soul, still encased in its causal and astral bodies, retires at physical death to continue its spiritual education and evolution until it incarnates again on earth.

the mystery of life you must be born anew every day. This means you must strive daily to improve yourself in some way. Above all, pray for wisdom, because with wisdom everything else comes. Be controlled not by moods, but by wisdom. And with that wisdom, develop creative thinking and activity. Keep busy doing constructive things for your own self-improvement and for the benefit of others, for whoever would enter God's kingdom must try also to do good for others every day. If you follow this pattern, you will feel the mood-dispelling joy of knowing you are advancing, mentally, physically, and spiritually. You will surely reach God, for that way leads to the kingdom of heaven.

Strive continuously to overcome moods; for as soon as you feel moody, you are cultivating seeds of error in the soil of your soul. To indulge in moods is to die gradually; but if you try daily to be cheerful in spite of any upsetting experiences, you will have a new birth. Until this human birth becomes transmuted into a highly spiritual birth, you cannot be "born again"* in God.

Moods are "catching," and at times of general depression can affect large numbers of people. Man should not take life's unhappy incidents so seriously. It is better to laugh a little than to make a tragedy of every misfortune. The Gita teaches: "He is dear to me who feels no distinction between the glad and the sad (aspects of phenomenal life), who is free from grief and cravings, and who has banished (the relative consciousness of) good and evil."† To have an optimistic disposition and try to smile is constructive and worthwhile; for whenever you express

---

* A *dvija,* one twice born. "Except a man be born again, he cannot see the kingdom of God....Ye must be born again" (John 3:3,7).
† Bhagavad-Gita XII:17.

divine qualities, such as courage and joy, you are being born again; your consciousness is being made new by the manifestation of your true soul nature. This is the spiritual rebirth that enables you to "see the kingdom of God."

Developing Personality

Self-Realization Fellowship International Headquarters, Los Angeles, California, October 28, 1938

Personality and its development are generally considered only in the light of realizing some material goal, such as increasing one's business or social opportunities. The real nature of personality is rarely analyzed.

What, essentially, *is* personality? It is the ego consciousness; not ego in the sense of inflated pride, but as the consciousness of existence. Each one of us knows: "I exist."

Further, we are conscious of existing in a certain way, as a man or a woman, and with certain characteristic qualities. We think about ourselves in terms of our individual background, experiences, and environment. A housekeeper thinks of herself as a housekeeper, a lecturer thinks of himself as a lecturer, a scientist thinks of himself as a scientist. Yet when they are asleep they forget their daytime activities. In sleep the consciousness of existence remains, though the egoistic concept of the wakeful personality may fade away entirely. But as soon as one awakens he remembers and becomes reassociated with his environmental identity. Therefore the personality a man displays in his wakeful hours is merely a cultivated and partial individuality.

The consciousness of existence is fundamentally a universal, unlimited state; but it becomes more or less bound by the personality traits that we hold to from day to day. Eventually we forget that our individual qualities can be expanded or contracted, according to our behavior.

Whence does our true personality derive? It comes from God. He is Absolute Consciousness, Absolute Existence, and Absolute Bliss. The Creator knows that He exists; He also knows that His existence is eternal, and that His nature is ever-new Bliss.

With the human mind we cannot know the Infinite Mind or perceive what ineffable Spirit is; but through the superconsciousness of the soul we can taste the Divine Presence as Bliss. The joy we receive from any experience flows from God, even though it may have been roused by some outward circumstance.

By concentrating within, you can directly feel the divine bliss of your soul within and also without. If you can stabilize yourself in that consciousness, your outer personality will develop and become attractive to all beings. The soul is made in God's image, and when we become established in soul awareness, our personality begins to reflect His goodness and beauty. That is your real personality. Any other characteristics you display are more or less a graft — they are not the real "you." The divine man, living in the cosmic consciousness of God, can assume any kind of outer personality he wishes.

When I am conscious of my human personality I have limitations, but as soon as I change my consciousness to the soul sphere I see everything just as if it were a motion picture. A person concentrating on the beam by which images are shown on a movie screen can see that all those figures are scintillating by the current of light emanating from the projector. In the same way, I see the world and all its creatures solely as

Developing Personality

projected thoughts of God. Concentrate on matter and you see everything in terms of matter. But as soon as you lift up your consciousness to the state of divine awareness, you see the oceanic current of God's light flowing behind all matter. You see everything in terms of Spirit.

Though the unity of God is reflected in everything, it appears diversified in cosmic nature. His creative life flows throughout the earth; put a seed in the ground and it begins to grow. Metals express a certain power and beauty of God. In the vegetable kingdom He changes His personality again; the active expression of life is more visible in plants. Still, a study of creation reveals that every metal, every plant, every animal has a distinctive personality; and in man we find an even more expanded individuality, for man *knows* that he is a living, conscious being. But all these different personalities have been borrowed from God; He is the only Life. "O Arjuna! I am the Self in the heart of all creatures; I am their Origin, Existence, and Finality." Thus the Lord describes Himself in the Gita.* And in the Bible we read this declaration: "I am Alpha and Omega, the beginning and the ending, saith the Lord, which is and which was, and which is to come, the Almighty."†

Intuition Develops One's True Personality

Our soul intuition is a faculty of God. He has no mouth, yet He tastes everything. He has no hands or feet, yet He feels the whole universe. How? By intuition, by His omnipresence.

Man ordinarily relies upon his senses to supply him with information about himself and the world in which he lives. His

---

* Bhagavad-Gita X:20.
† Revelation 1:8.

mind doesn't know anything except what his five senses tell him. But the superman relies upon intuition, his "sixth sense," for knowledge. Intuition doesn't depend on the senses or the power of inference for its data. For example, you feel certain that something is going to happen, and it does happen, exactly as you foresaw it. Each one of you has probably had some such experience. How did you know without any inferential or sense data? That direct knowing is the soul's power of intuition.

The ancient Indian sage Patanjali tells us that scriptural authority is not in itself proof of truth. How then can you know that the Bible and the Gita are true? The data relayed by the senses and the power of inference cannot give final proof. Truth is ultimately understood or "proved" solely by intuition, soul realization.

Your true personality begins to develop when you are able, by deep intuition, to feel that you are not this solid body but are the divine eternal current of Life and Consciousness within the body. That is how Jesus could walk on the water. He realized that everything is composed of the consciousness of God.

Human personality can be changed to divine personality. Banish the consciousness that you are a bundle of flesh and bones. Every night God makes you forget that delusion. But as soon as you wake up you are back again in the seeming confinements of the body.

Man Can Be Whatever He Wants to Be

Man can change his outer and inner nature by concentration. A person of strong mind can be whatever he wants to be. The limited human personality can be greatly expanded by meditation. When you close your eyes and feel the vastness of

Developing Personality

the soul within you, and when you can make that consciousness enduring, then you will have the personality that God intended you should have. The experience of the wakeful state has become predominant in your consciousness. But at the time of deep sleep, when man is granted freedom from the limitations of the flesh, you are in touch with Truth, with your real personality. Your attitude changes with the subconscious and superconscious realization: "I am Infinite. I am a part of everything."

As your consciousness expands with divine understanding, your personality becomes increasingly attractive and powerful. When your character grows in a spiritual way, you can assume almost any shade of personality you desire. Mind is illimitable; and as you develop spiritually and your inner life becomes separate from body consciousness, you no longer feel any egoistic attachment to the flesh; you are aware of ineffable freedom.

You shouldn't identify yourself as any particular type of individual. Rather be able to change your personality whenever you want to. I have done many different things in my life, just for the fun of it. I have invested money, I have done the work of a musician, of a contractor, of a cook. Truly, you can accomplish anything if you do not accept limitations by identifying yourself with your present personality. When you say to me that you can't do this or that, I don't believe it. Whatever you make up your mind to do, you can do. God is the sum total of everything, and His image is within you. He can do anything, and so can you, if you learn to identify yourself with His inexhaustible nature.

No matter if you have health and wealth and everything else

you want of the world, still there will always be some disillusion that will bring grief. Nothing of the earth is lasting; only God is lasting. When you develop the individuality that is an expression of His presence within you, which is your true Self, you will be able to attract anything you want. Any other personality you try to develop — whether that of an artist or a businessman or a writer — will bring disenchantment in its wake, because all human expressions have their limitations. You may go after success or money or fame, and achieve it; but always some flaw — lack of health or insufficient love or something else — will hurt you. The best course is to pray: "Lord, make me happy with awareness of Thee. Give me freedom from all earthly desires, and above all give me Thy joy that outlasts all the happy and sad experiences of life."

Never Forget Your True Nature!

Remember that as a child of God you are endowed with greater strength than you will ever need to overcome all the trials that God may send you.

Often we continue to suffer without making an effort to change; that is why we don't find lasting peace and contentment. If we would persevere we would certainly be able to conquer all difficulties. We must make the effort, that we may go from misery to happiness, from despondency to courage.

It is necessary first to feel the importance of changing our condition. This attitude stimulates our will to action. Let us resolve that we will always make an effort to improve our Self-knowledge and thus continuously better our existence.

India's spiritual scientists explored the kingdom of the soul. They have given to mankind for its benefit certain universal laws of meditation by which real seekers — those who wish to find a good life by changing themselves — may scientifically control their minds and attain Self-realization.

When you develop your divine nature you become completely detached about the body; you no longer feel identified with it. You look after it as you would attend to a little child. As you realize your true Self more and more, by meditation, you become freed from mental and physical pains. You cast off your lifelong limitations. That is the best way to live out your days on earth.

Awaken Your Divine Personality

Remember that it is not harmful to own things, but it is harmful to be owned by them. It is difficult to have the right balance. Struggling too hard for money, you may neglect your health. You will find that everything will betray you if you betray your loyalty to God. So let not one drop of oil fall from the lamp of your attention in the sanctuary of inner silence as you meditate each day, and as you carefully perform your duties in the world.* That is the personality you want to

---

* A story oft-related in India tells of the spiritual test given by the great saint, King Janaka, to his would-be disciple, Sukadeva. To test the young devotee before accepting him for spiritual training, Janaka required Sukadeva to tour the royal palace while carrying in the palm of his hand an oil lamp filled to the brim. The condition of passing the test was that Sukadeva was to observe minutely (and subsequently report to the King) every item and detail in each palatial room, without spilling one drop of oil from the brimful lamp. The meaning of the test is that the spiritual aspirant must learn to keep his attention centered in God, not allowing his thoughts to wander from Him for a moment, lest the oil of divine communion be spilled, while at the same time he performs accurately to the last detail his duties in the world.

develop — dutiful in carrying out your obligations in life, but aware that your real Home lies within. What is the use of developing a personality based on worldly values, which are ever changeful and fleeting? Rather strive for a personality that is derived from your living in the continuous consciousness of God. Bhagavan Krishna said: "When a man completely relinquishes all desires of the mind, and when his Ego (self) is entirely contented in the true Self, he is then considered to be one who is settled in wisdom."*

Awaken that meek yet thunderous divine personality — strong as the lion, gentle as the dove. When you make up your mind that you will meditate and follow this path, nothing will be able to take you away from it. Perform your worldly tasks faithfully, without forgetting for a moment your highest duty, to God.

* Bhagavad-Gita II:55.

Eliminating the Static of Fear from the Mind Radio

First Self-Realization Fellowship Temple at Encinitas, California, October 16, 1938

Everything in the universe is composed of energy, or vibration. The vibration of words is, by extension, a grosser expression of the vibration of thoughts. The thoughts of all men are vibrating in the ether.* Because thoughts have such a high vibratory rate, they have not yet been detected there; but it is fortunate that we do not know the thoughts of all men.

Through the instrumentality of radio, you can push a button and lo, you hear music and voices! If it were not for the intelligence in the ether, through which the radio waves travel to your receiving set, you might hear all the different broadcasts at once. God created the ether, and He planned that man would create radio and radio-wave vibrations which could be transmitted and received through this medium. Radio waves depend on the ether for transmission, and on electricity for amplification in broadcasting and receiving. The sounds of radio broadcasting are always present in the ether, but are inaudible to us without a radio instrument. The vibratory

---

* The hypothetical ether is not considered necessary to present scientific theory on the nature of the material universe. But Hindu scriptures refer to ether as a fine vibratory "background" on which creation is superimposed. It fills all interstices of space, and is the vibratory force that separates all images, one from the other. *(Publisher's Note)*

radio-waves represent thoughts that are being transmitted through space into any receiving set that is tuned in.

When you are near and dear to someone, you can feel the thoughts of that person; but you are probably not able to do this with anyone as far away as India unless you have developed range. Those of you who practice regularly the *Yogoda Satsanga Lessons* on concentration and meditation, and are very calm, will be able to feel the thoughts of others, even from a distance. Your mind will become more sensitive.

We are all human radios: you receive the thought messages of others through your heart,* the center of feeling, and broadcast your own thought messages through the spiritual eye, the center of concentration and will. Your antenna is in the medulla, the center of intuitive superconsciousness. Suppose you are away from home and you wish to perceive what is happening there. If your feelings are very calm and your mind quiet, you will be able to intuit the feelings and thoughts of your family at home. When you become capable of great concentration, your feeling can penetrate everywhere; your perception becomes charged with energy, with electricity.

The World Is Only a Thought in the Mind of God

There is in reality no space† between India and here. But we are in America and we think we have to allow twenty-five days

---

* The occult seat, in man, of *chitta*, intuitive feeling.
† Space and time are a part of the delusion of *maya*, which, to the perception of mortals, divides and measures the indivisible Infinite. In God's consciousness, which is untouched by *maya*, and to the devotee united with God in divine awakening, near and far, past, present, and future, all dissolve in the eternal omnipresent Now.

for a steamer trip before we can reach India. According to material consciousness time is required to traverse such a distance. But energy cuts down space. If we go by airplane, the trip takes but seven days.* The distance is decreased by the increased energy of flight — the more energy, the more reduction of space or distance. Suppose you are sleeping and you dream that you are going to India. You take the train to New York, board the boat, stop at various ports of call, and arrive in Bombay. All this can be done in minutes in the dream, because in thought there is no space. Or suppose I am dreaming that I am dialing a radio and I tune in India. There is no space; it is all an idea in my brain.

The whole world exists only in thought, such is the power of mind. Space is a mental concept. I can close my eyes and think of things that are two thousand miles away, and yet all those miles are a mere expansion of thought. Space and time are merely differentiations of thought. What is the difference between ice cream and hot coffee in a dream experience? When you awaken, you realize that in the dreamland ice cream was one thought and hot coffee another; they were merely two different ideas.

Thought has omniscient power. The kind of thought I am speaking of is the thought of God. As He is omnipresent through thought, so are we. Are we not already connecting the thought of America and the thought of India by radio? There is no space there.

---

* Seven days in 1938, and today a complete earth orbit in a matter of minutes by a spaceship! Time and space already have been greatly bent to the will of man. "Tomorrow" he may conquer them. *(Publisher's Note)*

Often when you are trying to tune in a radio station, static comes in and disturbs the program you are trying to hear. Likewise, when you are trying to accomplish some personal transformation in your heart, "static" may interrupt your progress. That static is your bad habits.

Fear Cannot Enter a Quiet Heart

Fear is another form of static that affects your mind-radio. Like good and bad habits, fear can be both constructive and destructive. For example, when a wife says, "My husband will be displeased if I go out this evening; therefore I won't go," she is motivated by loving fear, which is constructive. Loving fear and slavish fear are different. I am speaking of loving fear, which makes one cautious lest he hurt someone unnecessarily. Slavish fear paralyzes the will. Family members should entertain only loving fear, and never be afraid to speak truth to one another. To perform dutiful actions, or sacrifice your own wishes out of love for another person, is much better than to do so out of fear. And when you refrain from breaking divine laws, it should be out of love for God, not from fear of punishment.

Fear comes from the heart. If ever you feel overcome by dread of some illness or accident, you should inhale and exhale deeply, slowly, and rhythmically several times, relaxing with each exhalation. This helps the circulation to become normal. If your heart is truly quiet you cannot feel fear at all.

Anxieties are awakened in the heart through the consciousness of pain; hence fear is dependent on some prior experience — perhaps you once fell and broke your leg, and so you learned to dread a repetition of that experience. When you dwell on such an apprehension your will is paralyzed, and your nerves also, and you may indeed fall again and break your leg. Furthermore, when your heart becomes paralyzed by fear, your vitality is low and disease germs get a chance to invade your body.

Be Cautious But Not Fearful

There is hardly anyone who does not fear disease. Fear was given to man as a cautionary device to spare him pain; it is not meant to be cultivated and abused. Overindulgence in fear only cripples our efforts to ward off difficulties. Cautious fear is wise, as when, knowing the principles of right diet, you reason, "I won't eat that cake, because it is not good for me." But unreasoning apprehension is a cause of disease; it is the real germ of all sickness. Dread of disease precipitates disease. Through the very thought of sickness you bring it on yourself. If you are constantly afraid of catching a cold, you will be more susceptible to it, no matter what you do to prevent it. Do not paralyze your will and nerves with fear. When anxiety persists in spite of your will, you are helping to create the very experience you are dreading. Also, it is unwise to associate more than is necessary and considerate with people who constantly discuss their own and others' ailments and infirmities; this dwelling on the subject may sow seeds of apprehension in your mind. Those who are worried they are going to succumb to tuberculosis, cancer, heart trouble, should cast out this fear, lest it bring about the unwelcome condition. Those who are already sick and infirm need as pleasant an environment as possible, among people who have a strong and positive nature, to encourage them in positive thoughts and feelings. Thought has great power. Those who serve in hospitals seldom fall ill, because of their confident attitude. They are vitalized by their energy and strong thoughts.

For this reason, as you get older, it is best not to tell others your age. As soon as you do, they see that age in you and associate it with diminishing health and vitality. The thought of advancing age creates anxiety, and thus you devitalize yourself. So keep your age private. Say to God: "I am immortal. I am blessed with the privilege of good health, and I thank Thee."

Therefore be cautious, but not fearful. Take the precaution of going on a purifying diet now and then, so that any conditions of illness that may be present in the body will be eliminated. Do your best to remove the causes of illness and then be absolutely unafraid. There are so many germs everywhere that if you began to fear them you would not be able to enjoy life at all. Even with all your sanitary precautions, if you could look at your home through a microscope you would lose all desire to eat!

Techniques of Tuning Out Fear

Whatever it is that you fear, take your mind away from it and leave it to God. Have faith in Him. Much suffering is due simply to worry. Why suffer now when the malady has not yet come? Since most of our ills come through fear, if you give up fear you will be free at once. The healing will be instant. Every night, before you sleep, affirm: "The Heavenly Father is with me; I am protected." Mentally surround yourself with Spirit and His cosmic energy and think: "Any germ that attacks me will be electrocuted." Chant "*Aum*" three times, or the word "God." This will shield you. You will feel His wonderful protection. Be fearless. It is the only way to be healthy. If you commune with God His truth will flow to you. You will know that you are the imperishable soul.

Whenever you feel afraid, put your hand over your heart, next to the skin; rub from left to right, and say, "Father, I am free. Tune out this fear from my heart-radio." Just as you tune out static on any ordinary radio, so if you continuously rub the heart from left to right, and continuously concentrate on the thought that you want to tune out fear from your heart, it will go; and the joy of God will be perceived.

Fear Ceases with the Contact of God

Fear is constantly haunting you. Cessation of fear comes with the contact of God, nothing else. Why wait? Through Yoga you can have that communion with Him. India has something to give you that no other nation has ever given. I owe everything to my guru, Swami Sri Yukteswar; he was a master in every way. It was by following his wisdom that I was able to succeed in my mission in the West. He said, "Whatever you do, try to do it as nobody else has done it before." If you remember that thought, you will succeed. Most people imitate others. You should be original, and whatever you do, do well. All nature consciously communes with you when you are in tune with God.

We often consider ourselves first, but we should always include others in our happiness. When we do that from the goodness of our hearts, we spread abroad a spirit of mutual consideration. If everyone in a community of one thousand persons behaved this way, each one would have nine hundred and ninety-nine friends. But if everyone in that community behaved like an enemy to the other, each one would have nine hundred and ninety-nine enemies.

Conquering the hearts of others by the power of love is the greatest victory you can win in life. Always try to consider others first and you will find the whole world at your feet. That was the greatness of Jesus. He lived and died for all. Men of great material power who live only for themselves are soon forgotten, but those who live completely for others are remembered forever. The King of Kings had no throne of gold during his brief span on earth; but he has reigned for twenty centuries on a throne of love in the hearts of millions of people. That is the best throne to have.

A Single Thought May Lead to Redemption

When you came into this world you cried, whereas everyone else rejoiced. During your lifetime, work and serve in such a way that when it is time for you to leave this world, you will smile at parting while the world cries for you. Hold this thought and you will always remember to consider others before yourself.

This vast world was made that you might use your intelligence to acquire knowledge of the Spirit, knowledge about your Self. *Just one thought may redeem you.* You don't realize how effectively your thoughts work in the ether.

How would you know human love if God Himself didn't give it to you by planting His love in the heart of each being? And since God is so kind and so loving, then He should be the object of your search. He doesn't want to impose Himself on you. But the mysterious working of your body, the intelligence He has given you, and every other wonder in life should be sufficient stimulus to make you determine to find

Eliminating the Static of Fear from the Mind Radio

God. Every human being would be redeemed if he would try. You must try!

When I started in this path, my life at first was chaotic; but as I kept on trying, things began to clear up for me in a marvelous way. Everything that happened showed me that God *is*, and that He can be known in this life. When you find God, what assurance and fearlessness you will have! Then nothing else matters at all, nothing can ever make you afraid. Thus did Krishna exhort Arjuna to face fearlessly the battle of life and become spiritually victorious: "Surrender not to unmanliness. It is unbecoming of thee. O scorcher of foes, forsake this small weak-heartedness and arise!"*

* Bhagavad-Gita II:3.

Paramahansa Yogananda:
A Yogi in Life and Death

Sri Sri Paramahansa Yogananda entered *mahasamadhi* (a yogi's final conscious exit from the body) in Los Angeles, California, on March 7, 1952, after concluding his speech at a banquet held in honour of H.E. Binay R. Sen, Ambassador of India.

The great world teacher demonstrated the value of yoga (scientific techniques for God-realization) not only in life but in death. Weeks after his departure his unchanged face shone with the divine luster of incorruptibility.

Mr. Harry T. Rowe, Los Angeles Mortuary Director, Forest Lawn Memorial-Park (in which the body of the great master is temporarily placed), sent Self-Realization Fellowship a notarized letter from which the following extracts are taken:

"The absence of any visual signs of decay in the dead body of Paramahansa Yogananda offers the most extraordinary case in our experience....No physical disintegration was visible in his body even twenty days after death....No indication of mold was visible on his skin, and no visible desiccation (drying up) took place in the bodily tissues. This state of perfect preservation of a body is, so far as we know from mortuary annals, an unparalleled one....At the time of receiving Yogananda's body, the Mortuary personnel expected to observe, through the glass lid of the casket, the usual progressive signs of bodily decay. Our astonishment increased as day followed day without bringing any visible change in the body under observation. Yogananda's body was apparently in a phenomenal state of immutability....

"No odour of decay emanated from his body at any time....The physical appearance of Yogananda on March 27th, just before the bronze cover of the casket was put into position, was the same as it had been on March 7th. He looked on March 27th as fresh and as unravaged by decay as he had looked on the night of his death. On March 27th there was no reason to say that his body had suffered any visible physical disintegration at all. For these reasons we state again that the case of Paramahansa Yogananda is unique in our experience."

AIMS AND IDEALS
of
Yogoda Satsanga Society of India

As set forth by
Sri Sri Paramahansa Yogananda, Gurudeva and Founder
Sri Sri Mrinalini Mata, Sanghamata and President

To disseminate among the nations a knowledge of definite scientific techniques for attaining direct personal experience of God.

To teach that the purpose of life is the evolution, through self-effort, of man's limited mortal consciousness into God Consciousness; and to this end to establish Yogoda Satsanga temples for God-communion, and to encourage the establishment of individual temples of God in the homes and in the hearts of men.

To reveal the complete harmony and basic oneness of original Yoga as taught by Bhagavan Krishna and original Christianity as taught by Jesus Christ; and to show that these principles of truth are the common scientific foundation of all true religions.

To point out the one divine highway to which all paths of true religious beliefs eventually lead: the highway of daily, scientific, devotional meditation on God.

To liberate man from his threefold suffering: physical disease, mental inharmonies, and spiritual ignorance.

To encourage "plain living and high thinking"; and to spread a spirit of brotherhood among all peoples by teaching the eternal basis of their unity: kinship with God.

To demonstrate the superiority of mind over body, of soul over mind.

To overcome evil by good, sorrow by joy, cruelty by kindness, ignorance by wisdom.

To unite science and religion through realization of the unity of their underlying principles.

To advocate cultural and spiritual understanding between East and West, and the exchange of their finest distinctive features.

To serve mankind as one's larger Self.

Books and Audio Recordings by Sri Sri Paramahansa Yogananda

BOOKS BY PARAMAHANSA YOGANANDA

* Autobiography of a Yogi (*MP3 Audiobook, read by Ben Kingsley*)
* Autobiography of a Yogi
* Man's Eternal Quest
* The Divine Romance
* Journey to Self-realization
* The Science of Religion
* Whispers from Eternity
* Sayings of Paramahansa Yogananda
* Scientific Healing Affirmations
* Metaphysical Meditations
* The Law of Success
* How You Can Talk With God
* Where There Is Light
* God Talks With Arjuna: *The Bhagavad Gita* *(A New Translation and Commentary)*

AUDIO RECORDINGS OF PARAMAHANSA YOGANANDA

* Beholding the One in All
* Awake in the Cosmic Dream
* The Great Light of God
* To Make Heaven on Earth
* In the Glory of the Spirit
* Be a Smile Millionaire
* Chants and Prayers
* Songs of My Heart
* One Life Versus Reincarnation
* Removing All Sorrow and Suffering

OTHER BOOKS FROM YOGODA SATSANGA SOCIETY

* The Holy Science *by Sri Sri Swami Sri Yukteswar Giri*
* Only Love *by Sri Sri Daya Mata*
* Finding the Joy Within You: Personal Counsel for God-Centered Living *by Sri Sri Daya Mata*
* God Alone: The Life and Letters of a Saint *by Sri Gyanamata*
* "Mejda": Sri Sri Paramahansa Yogananda—His Family and Early Life *by Sananda Lal Ghosh*

Some of the above-mentioned books are also published in Bengali, Gujarati, Hindi, Kannada, Marathi, Malayalam, Nepali, Marathi, Oriya, Tamil, Telugu, and Urdu. For a complete list of books and audio recordings, write to Yogoda Satsanga Society of India at the address given below:

Yogoda Satsanga Society of India
Paramahansa Yogananda Path, Ranchi 834 001, Jharkhand
Tel. (0651) 2460071, 2460074, 2461578
www.bookstore.yssofindia.org

Also Published by Yogoda Satsanga Society of India

Autobiography of a Yogi
by Sri Sri Paramahansa Yogananda

This acclaimed autobiography is at once a riveting account of an extraordinary life and a penetrating and unforgettable look at the ultimate mysteries of human existence. Hailed as a landmark work of spiritual literature when it first appeared in print, it remains one of the most widely read and respected books ever published on the wisdom of the East.

With engaging candour, eloquence, and wit, Sri Sri Paramahansa Yogananda narrates the inspiring chronicle of his life — the experiences of his remarkable childhood, encounters with many saints and sages during his youthful search throughout India for an illumined teacher, ten years of training in the hermitage of a revered yoga master, and the thirty years that he lived and taught in America. He records as well his meetings with Mahatma Gandhi, Rabindranath Tagore, Luther Burbank, the Catholic stigmatist Therese Neumann, and other celebrated spiritual personalities of East and West. Also included is extensive material that he added after the first edition came out in 1946, with a final chapter on the closing years of his life.

Considered a modern spiritual classic, *Autobiography of a Yogi* offers a profound introduction to the ancient science of Yoga. It has been translated into twenty-six languages and is widely used in college and university courses. A perennial best-seller, the book has found its way into the hearts of millions of readers around the world.

"The Autobiography of this sage makes captivating reading."
— The Times of India

"A rare account." — The New York Times

"There has been nothing before, written in English or in any other European language, like this presentation of Yoga."
— Columbia University Press

Yogoda Satsanga Lessons

The *Yogoda Satsanga Lessons* are unique among Paramahansaji's writings in that they give his step-by-step instructions in yoga techniques for God-realization. The simple yet highly effective methods taught in the Lessons enable one to harmonize and recharge the body with life energy; to awaken the unlimited power of the mind; and, above all, to achieve direct, personal experience of God through the *Kriya Yoga* science of meditation.

In addition, the Lessons cover a broad range of other subjects — offering inspiration and practical guidance for living every day in greater harmony with oneself and others, and for coping with the multitude of problems that seem so pressing in today's world. A few of the many topics covered are:

- ✦ Strengthening the Power of Will for All-Round Success
- ✦ Freeing Yourself From Bad Habits
- ✦ Banishing Fear, Worry, & Stress
- ✦ Spiritualizing Business
- ✦ Finding & Expressing Unconditional Love
- ✦ Understanding Karma & Reincarnation
- ✦ Creating Harmony in Family Life & Marriage
- ✦ The Art of Getting Along With Others
- ✦ How to Weave God into Your Daily Life
- ✦ Life After Death
- ✦ How to Build World Unity
- ✦ Yoga Principles of Rejuvenation & Healing

For free Introductory Literature, please write or call:
YOGODA SATSANGA SOCIETY OF INDIA
Paramahansa Yogananda Path
Ranchi 834 001, Jharkhand
Tel. (0651) 2460071, 2460074, 2461578
www.yssofindia.org